Making Homemade Wine

by Robert Cluett

Wine is probably the most ancient and widespread alcoholic drink. It has been around at least several thousand years, as the literature of both the ancient Greeks and Hebrews tells us. Today, alcohol is available in a wide variety of forms: wines, beers, and distilled spirits. But it is wine that is the most popular with home brewers.

Wine is the easiest alcohol to make. It does not require the fastidious temperature control involved in brewing beer. Unlike distilled spirits, it requires no still and does not invite the curiosity of the revenue agents — unless you undertake to sell the wine you produce, and we do not recommend doing that. You can make fine wines from grapes or other fruits, or you can make it from vegetables, grains, or flowers.

This bulletin will take the mystery out of making wine. We will teach you the language of winemakers and explain what ingredients and equipment are essential to the process. We will offer some reliable and delicious wine recipes, and we will tell you the cure and prevention of 11 common problems — in case anything goes wrong with your wine. But we don't expect anything to go wrong. So, enjoy!

As with any speciality, winemaking has a language all its own. Before we go any further, let me introduce you to some of the terms you will come across in the text.

Champagning: The process of trapping carbonation into a still wine with a second, sealed ferment.

Cider: The customarily low-alcohol (6 to 9 percent) wine made from apples. Sometimes made sparkling, usually made still.

Fining: The removal of small-particle cloudiness from a wine.

Maderize: To cook a wine until it is like a Madeira. Wines stored at too high a temperature often will be said to be maderized.

Must: The dense liquid from which a wine begins. The point at which must stops being must and starts being wine is indefinite, but is generally conceded to be around SG (specific gravity) 1.030, or the point at which 60 percent of the sugar is converted into alcohol to give an alcoholic content of at least 7 percent.

Pearl: The carbon dioxide bubbles in a very slightly fermenting wine. Some wines, designed for a texture between champagne and still wine, are bottled when there is still a slight pearl in them.

Perry: Cider made from pears. See *cider.*

Plonk: A corruption of the French *blanc,* commonly used to denote a common white wine of French origin.

Rack: To siphon wine from one vessel to another.

Specific gravity: The density of a liquid as a fraction of the weight of water. A wine must with a lot of sugar in it will weigh between 8 percent and 12 percent more than water, hence will have a specific gravity (SG) of between 1.080 and 1.120. When these musts ferment out to the point where no sugar is left, they will give wines that weigh between 0.7 percent and 1.2 percent less than water (alcohol being lighter than water). The more alcoholic a finished dry wine is, the lower its SG.

Vinify: Literally, "to turn to wine."

Equipment

You do not need much equipment to make wine at home. Many of the items listed here may already be in your home. The rest should be available at any store that sells winemaking equipment. If there are no such stores in your area, you can order equipment from the suppliers listed in the back of this bulletin.

Essential Items

These are the pieces of equipment you will need to get started in home winemaking.

Air locks: These let carbon dioxide gas out of the carboy and prevent air from getting in. Buy one for each carboy.

Carboys: Large glass vessels used as secondary fermenters. Carboys hold 5 gallons of liquid. You need an extra empty carboy to rack wine into, so buy 1 more carboy than you plan to make batches of wine.

Funnel: Buy a large one.

Hose and J-tube: For siphoning and keeping the siphon level above that of the dead yeast in the bottom of the vessel.

Hydrometer set: Includes a hydrometer to measure the sugar content in the must and a tall tube.

Nylon bag: Select a fine-mesh or medium-mesh bag, measuring 2 feet by 2 feet. It is used with a mallet to make a homemade juice extractor.

Plastic sheet: To cover the vat.

Spoon: A long-handled wooden spoon works best; but a plastic one is an acceptable substitute. Used for stirring the must.

Strainer: Any large kitchen sieve will do.

String: Take a string that is 4 inches less than the circumference of your vat, and tie the ends to a 3-inch rubber band. Then you have an elastic tightener to hold the sheet on the vat.

Titration kit: Measures the acidity of the must.

Vat: You will need a large vessel, or vat, for the initial fermenting stage. I am partial to a 17-gallon garbage pail.

Helpful But Not Essential Items

Corker: For inserting corks in bottles.

Crown capper: Needed if you intend to make sparkling wines or ciders.

Crusher: Necessary for any large-scale operation that works directly from fresh fruit. It is not necessary for 10-gallon or 20-gallon batches. Crushers can be rented, but if you intend to go to press frequently you will probably want to own your own.

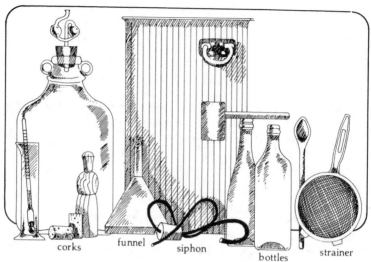

corks　　　funnel　　siphon　　　bottles　　strainer

Basic winemaking equipment

De-stemmer: For taking stems off fresh grapes. A large wooden spaghetti server makes an adequate substitute.

Filter and pump: These are used as a last-ditch method of clarification. I have used one once in 250 batches of homemade wine.

Gallon jugs: These are useful in the stage between carboy and bottle. Sometimes restaurants give them away.

Vinometer: Measures alcohol in wines that are fermented out and dry; it is not useful for wines with residual sugar in them.

Wine press: Device for pressing fruit either before or at the end of the first fermentation in the vat. It is necessary if you are making over 100 gallons a year of fresh grape or fresh fruit wine.

Ingredients

Listed below are the ingredients you will need, in addition to fruit, to make wine at home.

Essential Ingredients — Long Shelf-Lives

Acid blend: Raises acidity level of low-acid must and flabby finished wine.

Campden Tablets: Disinfects fresh must and wines during racking.

Disinfectant: Solution of water and potassium metabisulfite crystals, kept in gallon jug. Absolutely essential for cleanliness.

Grape tannin powder: Enhances the flavor and gutsiness of cider, perry, and wines made from concentrates.

Essential — But Perishable — Ingredients

Pectic enzymes: Removes the pectic haze from fruit wines and is put into the must just before yeast. It has a 3-month shelf life.

Yeast culture, liquid or powdered: Essential to fermentation, the yeast organisms turn sugar to alcohol. It has a one-year shelf life if kept unopened in the original sealed jar or packet.

Optional Ingredients

Finings: A powder used to remove microscopic particles that cloud wine.

Glycerine: Adds finish to table wines.

Oak chips: For adding barrel taste, especially to red wines.

Pure unflavored grain or grape alcohol: Fortifies port, sherry, and Madeira.

Sorbic acid (potassium sorbate): Stabilizes the wine before bottling.

Vitamin C tablets, 250 mg: Protects white wines from oxidation.

Basic Techniques of Winemaking

There are only 4 requirements for successful winemaking.

• *The weight or sugar content should be enough to read 1.060 to 1.080 on a hydrometer scale.* (All hydrometer readings in this book are given in the form of *specific gravity* (SG), that is, a fraction of the weight of water.)

• *The acidity of your must should measure .55 to .80 percent to prevent early deterioration.* Obtain this reading with your titration kit.

• *Proper temperatures must be maintained.* During the first 10 days of fermentation, the temperature of the must should measure at a maximum of 76 degrees F. for red wines and 70 degrees F. for fruit wines and white wines. The temperature of the must should never dip below 55 degrees F. Remember that a fermenting must will generate quite a bit of heat.

• *Absolute cleanliness.* This means keeping air out of contact with fermenting juice and wine, and it means meticulous sterilization of all equipment both before and after use. To sterilize equipment, use a sulfite solution made from crystals that are available from your wine-supply dealer.

Given these things, you need only a live yeast culture, some primitive equipment, and some patience in order to make good wine. We shall deal with all these things in detail — except, that is, the patience, for which I do not have the space or the time. As we go along, you will see that there is nothing complicated or even difficult about making wine.

There are 8 stages of winemaking, and we will take you through the first 7: preparation, primary fermentation, secondary fermentation, aging in the carboy, fining (an optional stage), finishing and bottling, and cellaring. Drinking the wine is the final stage, and you are on your own for that.

The processes we describe take days, weeks, and months. There is time to master each step as you go along. You will make your wine 1 stage at a time, beginning with the preparations.

Preparing the Equipment

Careful sterilization of all gear with a sulfite solution is essential. Here are a few rules for cleaning equipment.

• Never use detergent; use only a chlorine solution (and only for stains) and a sulfite solution, mixed in your own cellar with a gallon of warm water and a packet of crystals from a winemakers' supply store.

• Glassware should be rinsed inside with warm water first, then drained, then rinsed with sulfite solution. If the glassware is going to be stored, it should be stoppered with a small amount of solution in it (1/8 inch on the bottom). Bottles about to be used immediately *may* be rinsed again with water, but it is not necessary.

• Corks and screwcaps should be sterilized by a 60-second total immersion in sulfite solution; do not boil corks.

Winemaking:
Step by Step

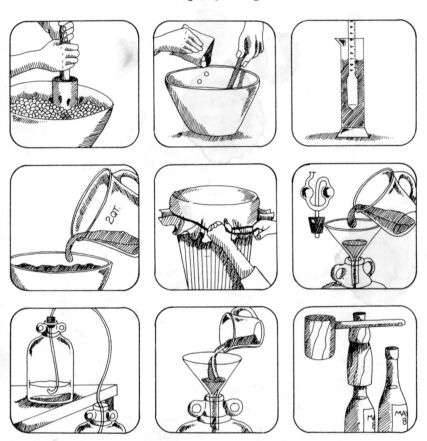

1. Wash the fruits, remove all stems and leaves. Then crush the fruit.
2. Add crushed Campden Tablets.
3. Test the must with a hydrometer and titration kit.
4. Add the yeast starter.
5. Cover the must tightly with a plastic sheet and secure it with a string.
6. When the weight of the must reaches SG 1.025 to 1.030, transfer the must to a carboy and fit the top with an air lock.
7. Rack the wine into a secondary fermenter.
8. Fine the wine with a special gelatin solution and rack again.
9. Bottle the wine.

- If fruit pulp sticks to your gear, use a *plastic* abrasive pad and hot water to remove it.
- When putting away your primary fermenters for a while, rinse with sulfite solution, cover with a plastic sheet, and secure with a tight string.

Preparing the Fruit

After you have removed all the stems and leaves from your washed fruit, it is ready for crushing. You can use a commercially available crusher for this stage, or you can improvise with a large plastic container and wooden mallet. With white grapes, as well as with many tree fruits, press out the vegetable matter in a press, so the must consists of nothing but juice. With red grapes, you will ferment first for 5 to 10 days and then go to the press. If you are making no more than 35 or 40 gallons a year, you can use a medium-mesh or fine-mesh nylon bag to get the effect of a pressing. Just crush your fruit in the bag, then squeeze the juice out.

The Garden Way cider press can be used to crush fruit for wine.

Add hot water and other ingredients (see recipe section) to the crushed fruit, and you will have a must, or a liquid that is nearly ready to ferment. Add to the must some Campden Tablets, which will keep it free from debilitating organisms.

Testing the Must

First, test the must with a hydrometer. If the must weight is between 1.080 and 1.095, you won't want to tinker. If it is below 1.080, you will want to add sugar; if it is above 1.095, you will probably want to cut the must somewhat with water, unless you want a very sweet or alcoholic wine. Temperature has a large effect on specific gravity readings, and hydrometers are calibrated to be accurate when the must is at 60 or 68 degrees F.

Next, test the must for acidity with a titration kit. If it is a red must and the acidity is .65 percent, or a white must and the acidity is .75 percent, you will be happy indeed. If your acidity is too low, add an acid blend (citric, malic, or tartaric). With shipped Califor-

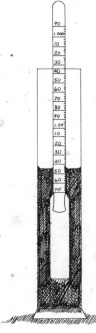

Measure specific gravity with a hydrometer. Some hydrometers are calibrated to read accurately at 60 degrees F., others at 68 degrees F. Make sure you are reading your hydrometer at the proper temperature. To read a hydrometer, ignore the way the liquid curves against the stem and tube because of surface tension, and take the reading from the level portion of the liquid.

nia grapes, the natural acidity will be too low. If it's too high (and with Eastern grapes, it may well be), you may want to cut the must somewhat with a sugar and water solution of weight 1.090, or with a dilute low-acidity must made from a hot-climate concentrate (also available from wine-supply stores). Some of my friends ferment their Eastern grapes at a natural acidity of 1.5 percent, but they are patient people: that kind of acidity level makes for either a disagreeable little wine or a long wait — about 5 years (wine loses acidity over time).

You can get to this stage of the process much more quickly and easily by using a grape concentrate from a winemakers' supply store or by using grape juice shipped to a juicer in your nearest urban area. You should not be put off by previous unhappy experiences with concentrates. In the last few years, Wine-Art Ltd. of Toronto, a marketer of home wine products, has been selling concentrates from Australia that make wines indistinguishable from those made with fresh grapes.

Adding the Yeast Culture

The last item of preparation is adding a yeast culture, which should have been mixed with a starter solution 2 to 3 days before the must was crushed or put together. Here is a formula for starting yeast for a 5-gallon batch of wine.

3 ounces frozen orange juice concentrate
24 ounces water
6 ounces sugar ⇐ 12 LEVEL T/S
2 rounded teaspoons of ordinary yeast nutrient

Put the frozen orange juice, water, and sugar into a 2-quart saucepan, and bring the mix to a boil on the stove. When the mix boils, remove it from the heat, add the nutrient, and cover the pot until the mix cools to room temperature.

Transfer the starter mix to a sterilized 1-gallon jug, add the yeast culture, and stopper the jug with an air lock. After 24 to 36 hours, "islands" of active yeast should appear on the surface of the liquid. Give the jug a swirl every 6 to 8 hours. When the solution gets to an active ferment (much CO_2 is expelled through the air lock when you swirl), it is ready to add to the must.

Always prestart your yeast for any batch of wine 3 gallons or more. The recipe given above will handle any quantity of wine from 3 to 12 gallons; for larger quantities you will want to double, triple or quadruple the recipe. For smaller quantities, add the yeast culture directly to the must from vial or packet, since the smaller quantities of must will dilute the culture less than larger ones.

Primary Fermentation

After you have adjusted weight and acidity, and added a yeast culture, the vat in which this first (primary) fermentation goes on should be covered with a tight-fitting plastic sheet, fastened with string. Once a vigorous, rolling ferment is started (24 to 48 hours), stir the must and push down the "cap" (the vegetable crust that will form on the top) twice a day. Use a well-sterilized wooden spoon.

Weigh the must every day after the third day, to see how rapidly the fermentation is going. A weight loss of .007 to .015 per day is good, more than that indicates that the must should be moved to a cooler place.

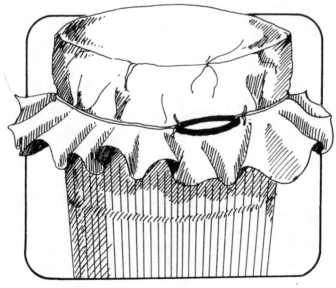

To secure the plastic sheet over the primary fermenter, I have invented an elasticized fastener I call "Cluett's String." I take a string that is 4 inches shorter than the circumference of my primary fermenter. Then, I tie the string to a 3-inch rubber band. This makes an easy-to-use string that secures a tight cover over the fermenter.

Test the must frequently with your best piece of winemaker's test equipment — your nose. The smell of a fermenting must is pervasive, at least in the space in which it is fermenting, sometimes throughout the house. If there is an aroma in addition to those of fruit and CO_2 coming from the wine, do not be disturbed unless that aroma has a strong sulphur or vinegar cast to it. In that case, turn to our troubleshooting section, pages 19 to 21.

When the weight reaches 1.025 to 1.030, transfer the wine to glass carboys with a siphon and J-tube. If you are making a red wine, press out the residual fruit left in the fermenting vat. (Here again, the nylon bag is a useful alternative to a press.) Stopper the carboys with air locks filled with sulfite solution to permit CO_2 to escape and prevent air contact with the wine. Leave the wine in the primary fermenter for 5 to 10 days.

Secondary Fermentation

The next step is to rack the wine into freshly disinfected carboys for the secondary fermentation. To rack wine from a primary to secondary fermenter, place the vessel with the wine in it on a shelf or table at least 30 inches high. Put the sterilized carboy or jug on the floor. Take a 5-foot or 6-foot length of clear tubing with a J-tube on the end, and place the J-tube into the wine, on the bottom of the vessel. Apply suction on the plastic hose to fill it, and put the discharge end quickly into the vessel you are filling. When the wine is completely transferred, rinse and sterilize both the used vessel and the plastic tubing. Change the disinfectant in the air locks.

Until you are very experienced, check the weight of your wine at this point, too. A weight of 1.005 to 1.010 will be average, though a wine that started off very heavy (1.100+) will be fermenting slower at this point because its high alcohol content will inhibit yeast action. A wine with a vigorous yeast in it may well be below 1.000. As long as the wine is sending even the occasional bubble up through the air lock, it is actively fermenting.

Aging

Rack your wine again in another 6 to 12 weeks, adding 1 crushed Campden Tablet per gallon. I prefer a 6-week interval, especially

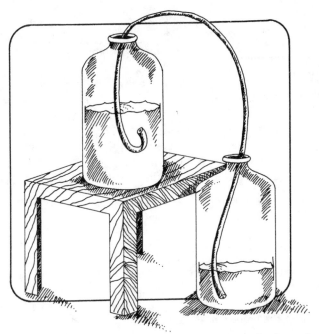

To rack the wine to a secondary fermenter, use a plastic J-tube and siphon the wine from the first carboy to the second. Keep the original carboy 30 inches higher than the fresh carboy. Be sure that the end of the tube is completely submerged in the wine. This arrangement prevents the wine from coming in contact with air.

with fruit wines. Three months after the second racking, you should rack again, adding more Campden Tablets. After this, rack every 6 months.

Change the disinfectant in the air locks every 3 months. SO_2 in solution is highly volatile, and fruit flies, which tend to carry vinegar bacteria on them, are massively persistent. Fresh disinfectant in the air lock is the best way to keep them out.

Fining

At the sixth month (perhaps even as soon as the sixth week with Cluett's Plonk, or the third month with some of the lower acidity wines from concentrate), you may want to fine your white wines.

Fining, the removal of small-particle cloudiness from a wine, was originally done with bull's blood or egg white, but both these items are messy. Far better to use a gelatin-based fining sold under several brand names. The most commonly used brand is Sparkalloid.

The special gelatin, in hot solution, is poured into a carboy of wine and coagulates around the small particles that cloud the wine, carrying them to the bottom of the carboy. After it has done its work completely (1 to 28 days), you can rack the clear wine off the fined gunk that has settled to the bottom of the vessel. The wine can then be stabilized (by adding 3/4 teaspoon of sorbic acid per gallon) and put into jugs or bottles, or simply left in the carboy to age further.

Finishing

Between the seventh and the twelfth month you will bottle most white wines, some reds, and most other fruit wines. Make sure that there is no threat of renewed fermentation in the wine; if that occurs after the wine is bottled, you will get some nasty explosions in your cellar.

Preventing renewed fermentation can be done in either of 2 ways. One way is to keep the wine under an air lock until it reaches a weight between .993 (for a starting weight of 1.080) and .990 (for a starting weight of 1.100), and not bottle before. This can involve an indefinite wait. Fermentation can stick at weights like .996 or .998, which indicate *some* residual sugar in the wine and probably *some* residual live yeast. Wines can sit for 18 and 24 months at .998 and then suddenly reignite after a change in the weather. It seems to me best to stabilize the wine by adding 3/4 teaspoon of sorbic acid (potassium sorbate) per gallon, whatever the weight of a wine when bottling.

There is an alternative to bottling: aging the wine in a gallon jug between carboy and bottle. With wines for which I have further plans, such as champagning, I use an air lock on the jug; other wines get 3/4 teaspoon of sorbic acid and a screw cap. Using the gallon jug has many advantages. With jug wines like Cluett's Plonk, bottling is just a chore. It is far preferable to have 4 wide-mouth, stoppered, 1-liter carafes that can be kept in the refrigerator. The wine will last nicely for 5 to 6 weeks. A further advantage is that the gallon jug leaves you flexibility for blending

Bottle capper

wines, especially reds. Some of your wines will be too dark, some too light, some too tannic, some too smooth (yes, *too* smooth, a forecast of short life). Such wines, so long as they do not taste outright bad, will often benefit from being blended with wines of opposite character. I keep a few gallon jugs of elderberry-enriched Petite Syrah on hand to give backbone and color to the pale, pale California Carignane of which I make a carboy or so each year.

At this point (seventh month) you will probably want to add a packet of oak chips (available from your wine-supply dealer) to your better reds for about a month. This process adds oak tannin and barrel flavor to the wine and is generally beneficial. To remove the chips, rack the wine again.

After the oaking, which you may want to do a second time on some wines, taste the wine for finish, or ability to hang on the palate. First, swirl an inch of wine around in a large wine glass. If it leaves several glycerine streaks down the side of the glass (so-called legs), you have a good sign. Second, put the wine into your mouth, squeeze it into the corners back of your teeth and under your tongue, and then swallow. If the flavor of the wine and its intensity last after swallowing, then you have a second and wholly convincing good sign. If the wine throws no or few legs, or if it quits quickly after being swallowed, then add 4 ounces of glycerine to the carboy and repeat the 2 tests about 8 weeks later, adding more glycerine if the wine is still unleggy or faint-hearted on the palate. Some time around the eighteenth month, stabilize and bottle your better reds.

Bottling

I always bottle and cork my better wines. Although some people swear by plastic screw caps, most serious amateurs prefer cork. Cork breathes slightly and allows the very *slow* process of oxidation that facilitates the aging of the wine. The better the wine, the more worthy it is of being placed under cork.

Do not use recycled corks. Use new, waxed corks from a reliable supplier. And, the better the wine, the longer the cork you will need; your cork should be at least 1-1/4 inches long, with a diameter slightly larger than that of the mouth of the bottle.

Before bottling, prepare the corks. Place them in water that just has been boiled (never boil the corks), cover the vessel, and leave

I always bottle and cork my better wines. You can use recycled glass soda bottles. These are some of the traditional bottle shapes. From left to right: Burgundy, sauterne, Rhine.

them for 5 minutes. Then place them in a sulfite solution, pushing them down in the solution to make sure they have been covered fully by the sulfite. Then they are ready to use, and you can siphon your wine into a sterilized bottle. Recycled *glass* — not plastic — bottles are okay, but make sure that they have been completely cleaned and rinsed with sulfite solution.

Many devices for driving home corks are available — from $2.00 wooden gadgets to $150.00 production-line devices. My own recommendation is the San-Bri handcorker from France, which retails for about $10.00 and is both quick and reliable. This corker has a metal collar for squeezing the cork and a piston for driving it home.

When you cork the wine, do not countersink the cork; keep it level with or slightly above the very top of the bottle opening. One further suggestion: If you use a hand corker of any kind, put the filled bottles into divided wine cases before corking them; this prevents the bottles from spontaneously overturning, spilling wine or breaking glassware.

As for putting a plastic or metal seal over the top and neck of the bottle, I do not recommend it. The capsule is strictly a decorative device, and it impedes the breathing of the cork.

Cellaring

After bottling, you are usually in for a wait of 6 months or more, possibly much more. Periodic checking is the key to timing the consumption of the wine at its peak point. Unless a wine is hideously astringent (in which case an annual check is enough), opening a new bottle every 6 months will be enough to keep you abreast of a wine's progress. You should always remember that patience can be a great healer of the problems of a wine. Several of my friends have produced wines they pronounced "undrinkable" at an early stage, only to see the wines turn highly drinkable some 3 to 5 years later. Don't give up too soon.

Much is made of "correct" storage and some of the myths are downright silly. There are, however, 4 basic rules for cellaring that have the force of sacred writ.

• Store wine away from light, especially direct sunlight or fluorescent fixtures; these kinds of light maderize wine, or make it go off in flavor.

• Store corked wines on their sides. If they are stored upright, the corks dry out, and air gets to the wine, ruining it eventually.

• Wine storage temperature should never go over 75 degrees F., except for brief spans of time. At 75 degrees F., wine begins to oxidize.

• Temperature in a wine storage area should be as steady as possible; changes should be gradual. A 68-degree to 73-degree F. storage area is far preferable to one whose range is 45 to 65 degrees F., even though the first one makes a closer approach to the dangerous 75-degree F. figure. Rises in temperature force wine through the cork; drops cause air to be sucked back in. The greater the changes in temperature a wine suffers, the greater the premature aging of the wine from overbreathing.

Follow these guidelines, and your cellar (or closet) will never ruin a well-made bottle of wine.

Day-to-Day Summary

The list below provides a day-by-day summary of all that I have described to this point.

Day 1	Start your yeast culture.
Day 3	Crush and de-stem the fruit. Add Campden Tablets. Weigh, test for acidity, adjust for sugar and acid balance. Press (white and most fruit wines), add yeast to the must in premixed starter.
Day 4 or 5	Break up the cap and stir. Do this daily thereafter until wine reaches a specific gravity of 1.030.
Day 10	(Or when the wine reaches a specific gravity of 1.030.) Press out the grapes in red wines. Rack all wines into carboys and stopper with air locks and sulfite.
Day 25	Rack into fresh carboys. Add Campden Tablets.
Month 3	Rack again, and again 3 months later, and every 6 months thereafter.
Month 7	(Or sooner.) Fine whites. Stabilize and bottle most whites, some reds. Red wines may be oaked.
Month 8	Check reds for finish. Add glycerine if needed.

Month 12	White wine bottled in month 7 is probably drinkable. Beaujolais from France and other light reds may also be ready to serve.
Month 18	Bottle better reds, wait minimum of 6 months to drink them.
Month 24 to year 40	Wines become drinkable and reach their age limits.

The rate of maturation, especially in red wines, will vary enormously with the style of vinification. You can vinify with the stems left on the grapes and get much more tannin and acidity into your wine; this will mean early harshness but longer life. Similarly, the more complete your pressing of the grapes, the more tannin, acid, and coloring matter will go into the wine. To vinify a red wine lighter, press sooner (but leave the wine in vat until its weight reaches 1.030), and press more lightly. Filtration, too, will make a lighter, faster-maturing wine.

Troubleshooting

Because each of us has a distinct style of going about things, we each will evolve a distinctive set of winemaking problems — and solutions for them. There are, however, certain problems that plague about 95 percent of the winemaking population. I have had all of them except mycoderma and vinegar, and these two I have suffered through vicariously with neighbors. What follows is a handy guide to the Universal Ills of Winekind, ordered by their probable place in the life of the wine.

1. *Stuck starter:* the yeast will not ignite. *The cause:* either the starter was too cool or the yeast too old. *The cure:* move the bottle to the top of the refrigerator or get new yeast. Prevent it next time by keeping the starter at a temperature of 68 to 72 degrees F., and deal only with a first-class supplier.

2. *Stuck ferment in the primary fermenter* (first week to 10 days) has 4 probable causes.

• If the must or wine gets too hot (above 76 degrees F.), the heat will kill the yeast. *The cure:* move to a cooler place; add freshly started yeast culture. Prevent it next time by watching the temperature carefully.

- If the must is too cool (under 58 degrees F.), the yeast will not ignite. *The cure:* move the must to a warmer place. Watch the temperature carefully.

- If the must is too heavy (SG 1.115 or more), the sugar will inhibit fermentation. *The cure:* cut the must with water and acid blend. To prevent it, add the sugar in stages, rather than at the beginning. (I presume in this case you want a wine that is alcoholic or sweet or both.)

- If there is not enough nutrient for the yeast, fermentation is inhibited. This is especially likely with blueberry, pear, and peach must. *The cure:* add nutrient and fresh yeast culture. Next time, use a good recipe and follow it exactly.

3. *Stuck ferment in the secondary fermenter* (carboy) can be caused by all of the above. There is also a chance that the wine sticks (often at SG 1.012) for causes that are utterly mysterious. *The cure:* add "supernutrient," a magnesium and vitamin B mix that gives you a stronger kick than the ordinary ammonia and uric acid nutrient. If that fails, add fresh yeast culture. If that fails, wait for the wine to clear, and add it in a 1 to 5 ratio to other wines that are in a healthy secondary fermentation. Otherwise, resign yourself to having made a sweet wine. Before you bottle this wine, stabilize it.

4. *Hydrogen sulfide* (rotten egg aroma) is a special threat to low-acid wines, notably Cluett's Plonk and any wine made from vinifera grapes that have been shipped a long distance. It is recognizable by the unmistakable aroma of rotten eggs, and it usually occurs in the second to fourth week of the wine's life — although I have had it happen in hot weather during the fifth day. The cause is dead yeast and dead fruit pulp working together in low-acid wine. *The cure:* pour the wine (do not siphon) into a fresh carboy with 1 Campden Tablet per gallon. Use a funnel and make sure the wine is well-aerated. This is the only exception to the general rule to keep air out of wine. The prevention is to rack more often and watch acidity levels.

5. *Mycoderma* appear as grey islands of organisms on the wine; they are caused by poor sanitation. *The cure:* immediately strain the wine through fine cotton mesh and add 2 Campden Tablets per gallon. Once mycoderma have covered the entire surface of the wine, however, the wine is lost and must be thrown out. Prevent this by keeping your equipment sterilized and keeping air out of your wine.

6. *Vinegar smell and taste* is caused by poor sanitation. There is absolutely no cure, the wine is lost. Next time, keep your equipment sterilized and keep air out of your wine.

7. *Browning* occurs in white wines from using overripe fruit or allowing the wine to be in contact with air. There is no real cure, but the browning can be halted by adjusting the acid balance, adding ascorbic acid (250 mg/gallon), and keeping air out. Prevent browning by avoiding overripe fruit and contact between wine and air.

8. *Stuck fining* happens when the wine is too warm or too low in acid. *The cure:* add 1 tablespoon of acid blend to the carboy, decrease the temperature by 5 degrees F. If this fails — and it will occasionally fail — rent a filter and pump from your friendly local supply house and use them. The next time, fine your wine at the proper temperature (65 degrees F. and under) and acidity (.06 or more).

9. *Explosion or spontaneous degorgement* is caused by residual sugar and live yeast in the wine when bottled. *The cure:* unbottle all remaining wine of that batch to a carboy, add potassium sorbate, and rebottle. Prevent this by reading the hydrometer carefully and stabilizing the wine before bottling.

10. *Bottle odor* when wine is opened has 2 causes.
- If there is a sulphur odor, it means there was too much sulfite in the bottle when it was filled. *The cure:* decant the wine an hour before drinking; leave the decanter unstoppered. The SO_2 will evaporate. Next time, when you bottle your wine, rinse the bottles with water after sterilizing them; or keep them upside down after sterilizing.
- A mildew odor probably indicates a rotten cork. Sometimes it is caused by mildewed fruit. There is no cure; but open 2 or 3 bottles from the same batch to see if all are affected. If all the bottles have a mildew taste in the wine, scrape the batch. If only some bottles have mildew in the wine, recork the sound bottles. Prevent this problem with strict attention to sanitation. Also, pick over your fruit and remove suspect berries before you crush.

11. *Undue harshness* is caused by too much acidity, tannin, youth, all 3, or any 2 thereof. *The cure:* patience, and blending with wine of opposite character. Give the wine at least a few months before blending. Prevent this by using the best suppliers you can find for your fruits and concentrates.

Recipes

In the best of all possible worlds, we would have 135 pages for recipes and would cover everything from apricots to zucchinis. Alas, we have had to be selective. The recipes were selected to cover cider, still wines, and champagne; the major kinds of materials (grape, other fruit, grain, and flower); and the tree and vine fruits most likely to come into the hands of home winemakers. If you are in possession of a material not specifically covered here (rice, for example), you can make a reasonable wine from the recipe in our group that is closest to your material. In the case of rice, for example, use the recipe for wheat.

By the way, we do not offer a specific recipe for grape wines. They have been covered both in the main text in some detail and in the Universal Recipe to be found on page 30.

Once you find that a recipe works reasonably well for you, you might find it interesting to try variations. For example, you can make a wine taste *drier* by adding a rounded teaspoon of acid blend per gallon. This, in fact, does not make the wine any drier (that is, lacking in sugar); it simply makes it more tart. You can make a wine *sweet* by starting with a SG of 1.115 or by stopping fermentation with sorbic acid at SG 1.002 to 1.005. You can give a wine *longer life* by adding extra tannin to the must before the yeast culture is added, or by the addition of stem, pip, or freeze-dried whole grapes. You can give a wine *more alcohol* by adding extra sugar to the must, preferably in stages after the fermentation has begun.

The recipes do not specify the amount of yeast needed. Here is the rule to follow. If you are making 3 gallons or less, simply add 1 packet or 1 vial of wine yeast culture to your must, when the must cools to 70 degrees F. or less. If you are making over 3 gallons, it is best to start your yeast in the way described on page 10, then add it to the cooled must.

Where fruit concentrates are called for, I have not specified the exact amounts for some of the other ingredients. You will find instructions for adding the proper amounts of tannin, yeast nutrients, water, pectic enzymes, and so on, on the concentrate labels.

We will not repeat our injunctions about keeping everything

absolutely sterile. In addition to this, it is a good protection to add a crushed Campden Tablet for each gallon of must at the beginning of fermentation, and to add an additional crushed Campden Tablet every second racking. When dealing with concentrates of juices, always ask the supplier about the need for Campden Tablets.

CLUETT'S PLONK

This makes an all-purpose dry white wine, ready to drink in 6 to 10 weeks.

1 unit (100 ounces) apricot concentrate
1 unit non-Labrusca white grape concentrate
corn sugar (75 percent of what is called for on concentrate labels)
grape tannin (as per labels)
yeast nutrient (as per labels)
acid blend (1-1/2 ounces less than combined total on labels)
warm water (as per labels)
yeast culture
pectic enzyme (as per labels)

Mix all the ingredients, except the yeast and pectic enzyme in a 17-gallon plastic vat. The water temperature should be 105 to 110 degrees F. Cover the vat with a plastic sheet secured with a string. Put the vat in a place that is room temperature (65 to 75 degrees F.). Wait 24 hours, then measure the specific gravity and adjust to 1.080. Add water if the SG is too high; add sugar if it is too low. Measure acidity, and adjust to .55 to .60 percent by adding acid blend or water. If you add water, add sugar also to bring SG to 1.080. When the acid and SG levels are satisfactory, add the yeast culture and pectic enzyme.

Rack into carboys 5 days after fermentation starts; rack again in 10 days. This wine, with its high pulp content and low acidity, is very vulnerable to hydrogen sulfide and must be racked often. That's bad news, but one does not get a ready wine this quickly without paying a price.

This recipe makes 2 5-gallon carboys or 50 bottles — almost a month's drinking.

FLOWER WINE

With honeysuckle and clover, some winemakers like to stabilize the wine with sorbic acid, then add sugar to SG 1.005 or 1.010 before bottling.

2 quarts flowers (dandelion heads, clover blossoms, or honeysuckle blossoms)
1/4 pound raisins, chopped
juice and peel of 2 oranges
juice and peel of 2 lemons
3 pounds sugar
1 ounce acid blend
1/4 teaspoon grape tannin
1 gallon boiling water
yeast culture

Gather the flowers on a dry, sunny day and make sure they are fully open. Remove the green parts, and put the flowers in a 2-gallon plastic vessel with the peel *only* of the oranges and lemons. Add boiling water. Cover the vat and secure, stirring the mixture every 12 hours to keep flowers saturated. After 4 days, strain off the liquid and press the pulp. Add to the liquid all the other ingredients, including the juice of the oranges and lemons, stirring well to dissolve the sugar. Adjust the must to SG 1.100. Ferment to SG 1.030, and remove to a gallon jug with air lock. Rack in 3 weeks, then in 3 months. When the wine is clear, stabilize and bottle.

This recipe makes 5 bottles or 1 gallon — all drinkable in a year.

APRICOT OR PEACH WINE

5 pounds apricots *or* peaches
1 gallon boiling water
2-1/4 pounds sugar
1 tablespoon acid blend
1/2 teaspoon yeast nutrient
1/2 teaspoon pectic enzyme
yeast culture

Stone the fruit and cut it up, placing it in a 2-gallon plastic vessel. Add the boiling water and steep for 2 days; strain out and press the fruit. Then add the sugar and acid blend. Adjust the must to SG 1.095. Then add the nutrient, pectic enzyme, and yeast, stirring well. Stir daily. At SG 1.030, remove to gallon jug with an air lock. Rack in 3 weeks, then at 3 months. When clear, stabilize and bottle. This recipe makes 1 gallon or 5 bottles.

CHAMPAGNE, COLD DUCK, AND CANADA GOOSE

The tax collectors, who levy heavier by far on bubbles than on alcohol, have made these wines much prized. Actually, the carbonic gas in such wines disguises true flavors, so champagning is an excellent expedient for wines that are free of mildew and vinegar, but still do not taste quite up to snuff.

For these sparkling wines, you will need 25 26-ounce pop bottles with crown cap tops and a capper.

1 5-gallon carboy of fully fermented wine that was started at SG 1.080 or
    less and has *not* been stabilized with sorbic acid
water
acid blend
10 ounces sugar
1 packet dry champagne yeast

If the wine you are using started at SG 1.090, add 1/9 of its volume in water, plus a level tablespoon of acid blend for each half gallon of water. If the wine you are using started at SG 1.095, add 1/6 its volume in water, plus acid blend at half a tablespoon per gallon of water.

Sterilize the bottles; then rinse them with plain water. In each bottle, place a rounded teaspoon of sugar and a few grains of the dry yeast. Fill the bottles to within 3 inches of the top. Cap with sterilized crown caps. Shake vigorously, and do so again on the seventh and thirtieth days. Before and after shaking, keep bottles upright.

After the thirtieth day, leave them for 2 months. At that point, remove a cap and check for fizz. If it's good, you can start drinking. If it's slightly torpid, you can start drinking anyway; but if you recap and wait another 90 days, your patience should be rewarded with more bubbles. This recipe makes 24 bottles or 2 cases, plus a test bottle.

Cluett's Plonk is an excellent champagne base; the bubbly from it has been compared by *cognoscenti* to the champagne made at Chateau Margaux. Another interesting base for bubbly is a mixture of 3 or 4 different carboy ends brought together in a gallon jug when you are bottling; for this, you need only 5 bottles, 2 ounces of sugar, and 5 crown caps. The end product has been called Cold Duck and Canada Goose in North America and Hegel's Synthesis in Eastern Europe.

CIDER OR PERRY

A festive drink, 7-1/2 percent alcohol, with a distinct pearl. Great for summer parties! To make this recipe you will need 5 26-ounce soda bottles and 5 crown caps.

3 pounds apples *or* pears
2 Campden Tablets
1 gallon boiling water
25 ounces sugar
3 teaspoons acid blend
1 teaspoon yeast nutrient
1/2 teaspoon grape tannin
1/2 teaspoon pectic enzyme
yeast culture

Remove stems from fruit, cut the fruit into quarters, and crush it in a large plastic vessel. Dissolve Campden Tablets in the boiling water, and pour the water over the fruit, stirring the mix well. Tightly cover the vat. After 72 hours, pour off the liquid and press out the fruit. Add the sugar, acid blend, nutrient, and tannin. Adjust the must to SG 1.060. Then add the pectic enzyme and yeast culture. Cover. Stir twice daily for 5 days or so, measuring the SG daily. At 1.030, transfer the fermenting must to a glass vessel with air lock.

Continue to measure the SG at 2-day to 3-day intervals, until it reaches 1.010. At that point, transfer the wine to sterilized *and* rinsed bottles, capping them with sterilized crown caps. The bottles should be filled to within 3 inches of the cap. Store the bottles upright. When the liquid is clear, the cider or perry is ready to drink. When serving, be careful not to disturb the sediment on the bottom of the bottle. This recipe makes 1 gallon or 5 bottles.

ELDERBERRY WINE

6 ounces dried *or* 3-1/2 pounds fresh elderberries
8 ounces raisins, chopped
2-1/2 pounds sugar
4 teaspoons acid blend (optional)
1 teaspoon nutrient
2 Campden Tablets
1 gallon hot water
1/2 teaspoon pectic enzyme
yeast culture
vitamin C tablets

Combine the elderberries and raisins in a primary fermenter and add the sugar, acid blend, nutrient, Campden Tablets, and hot water. Cover. When the mix has cooled to 70 degrees F., adjust the must to 1.100. Add the pectic enzyme and yeast culture. Cover with plastic sheet and secure with a string. Stir the must daily for 7 days. Strain out the fruit and siphon the liquid to a glass vessel with an air lock. *Do not press the fruit.* Pressed elderberries put out a hideous green gunk that ruins every piece of equipment with which it comes in contact. Beware.

Rack the wine in 3 weeks, again every 3 months. When the wine is clear and stable, bottle it, adding a 250 mg. vitamin C tablet per gallon. Makes 1 gallon or 5 bottles.

POTATO OR CARROT
OR PARSNIP WINE

4-1/2 pounds potatoes *or* carrots *or* parsnips
peel and juice of 2 oranges
peel and juice of 2 lemons
1 gallon boiling water
2-1/2 pounds sugar
1 teaspoon yeast nutrient
1/2 teaspoon pectic enzyme
1/2 teaspoon grape tannin
yeast culture

Scrub and dice the vegetables, removing the skins and all the discolored parts. Add the peel *only* of the fruit. Add the water and boil until the vegetables are tender. Let stand for 1 hour. Strain into a plastic vessel and add sugar. Cover. When the liquid is cool, add the other ingredients, including the juice of the oranges and lemons. (Some people at this point like to add ground ginger, ground cloves, and/or chopped raisins.) Adjust to SG 1.085. Stir daily for 5 days. Move to a glass vessel with an air lock. (If you added raisins, strain the wine first.) Rack in 3 weeks, again at 3 months. When the wine is clear, stabilize and bottle it. It will reach its peak of palatability in 6 to 15 months. Makes 1 gallon or 5 bottles.

APPLE OR PEAR WINE

8 pounds apples *or* pears
2 Campden Tablets
1 gallon boiling water
2 pounds sugar
juice of 2 lemons *or* 4 teaspoons acid blend
1 teaspoon yeast nutrient
1/2 teaspoon pectic enzyme
1/2 teaspoon grape tannin
yeast culture

Remove stems from the fruit, cut the fruit into quarters, and crush it in a large plastic vessel. Dissolve Campden Tablets in the boiling water, and pour the water over the fruit, stirring the mix well. Tightly cover the vat.

After 72 hours, pour off the liquid and press out the fruit. Add sugar, adjusting the SG to 1.090. Then add lemon juice (or acid blend), yeast nutrient, pectic enzyme, tannin, and yeast culture. Cover. Stir twice daily for 7 days. Remove to a glass vessel with an air lock. Rack in 3 weeks, again at 3 months. When the wine is clear, stabilize and bottle. This recipe makes 1 gallon or 5 bottles.

RASPBERRY OR PLUM WINE

This recipe will yield a dry and modest fruit wine of roughly 11 percent alcohol. Some rustics like both a more robust and a sweeter fruit wine. If you be one of these, increase the sugar to 3-1/2 pounds, adding it 2 pounds at the beginning, 1 pound on the fourth day, 1/2 pound on the sixth day.

- 3 pounds fruit, de-stemmed and de-stoned
- 2 teaspoons acid blend
- 2 Campden Tablets
- 2 pounds sugar
- 1 gallon warm water (100 degrees F.)
- 1 teaspoon yeast nutrient
- 1/2 teaspoon grape tannin
- 1/2 teaspoon pectic enzyme
- yeast culture

Crush the prepared fruit in a plastic vessel. Add all the ingredients, except the pectic enzyme and yeast. Stir thoroughly to dissolve the sugar. Cover with a plastic sheet. When the mix cools, adjust the must to SG 1.085. Add the pectic enzyme and the yeast culture. Cover and secure, stirring twice daily for 6 days. At that time, or whenever the must reaches SG 1.030, remove to a glass vessel and secure with an air lock. Rack in 3 weeks and again at 3-month intervals for 1 year; then stabilize and bottle the wine. This recipe makes 1 gallon or 5 bottles.

WHEAT WINE

Often a delight and a surprise. When made sweet — with 3-1/2 pounds of sugar — it can be a very nice dessert wine.

- 1 pound whole wheat berries
- 1-1/2 pounds raisins
- 1 gallon boiling water
- peel and juice of 1 lemon
- peel and juice of 2 oranges
- 2 pounds sugar
- 1/2 teaspoon acid blend
- 1/4 teaspoon grape tannin
- 1/2 teaspoon yeast nutrient
- 1/4 teaspoon pectic enzyme
- yeast culture

Crush the wheat, using a rolling pin and bread board, and add it with the chopped raisins to a 2-gallon vessel. Add boiling water, the peel *only* of the oranges and lemons, the sugar, the acid blend, tannin, and the nutrient. Move to a spot at room temperature.

When the mix cools, add the juice of the fruits. Adjust the SG to 1.100. Add the pectic enzyme, and the yeast culture. Cover and secure; stir daily for 5 days. After 7 days, strain (do not press) into a 1-gallon jug with air lock. Rack in 3 weeks and again in 3 months. Bottle the wine when it is clear and stable. Makes 5 bottles or 1 gallon.

UNIVERSAL WINE RECIPE*

We offer you here the universal wine recipe chart of Mr. Stanley F. Anderson, of Vancouver, B.C. You will find it handy at times when you have picked a large quantity of ripe fruit that you want to ferment before it spoils — or when a quantity or ripe fruit has been dumped on you by a zealous acquaintance. The steps you should take are as follows.

1. Get a vessel (preferably plastic) that holds about 1-1/2 times the volume of the crushed fruit. This can range from a 2-gallon plastic pail for 5 pounds of fruit to a 45-gallon plastic drum liner for 350 pounds of grapes.

2. Multiply or divide the quantities shown on the chart, and get the appropriate ingredients from a winemaker's supply house, if you do not already have them. Get Andovin yeast if you can, otherwise use some other high-grade winemaker's yeast, and prestart it as explained on page 10.

3. Prepare the fruit as indicated on the chart.

4. Mix all the ingredients, crushing the Campden Tablets before adding them, and stirring the must well to dissolve the added sugar. Put it in a place that is between 65 and 75 degrees F. Add the yeast culture.

5. Cover with a plastic sheet and secure with a string.

6. Stir twice a day and follow the steps outlined on pages 11 through 18.

---

*This recipe first appeared in *The Art of Making Wine* by Stanley Anderson and Raymond Hull (Longman).
Used with permission.

FRUIT	WEIGHT OF FRUIT TO YIELD 1 GALLON	PREPARATION OF FRUIT	WATER	ACID BLEND	CAMPDEN TABLETS	YEAST NUTRIENT	SUGAR	RAISINS	PECTIC ENZYME	GRAPE TANNIN	WINE YEAST
Apples	8 lb.	Crush	1 gal.	4 tsp.	2	1 tsp.	2 lb.	None	1/2 tsp.	1/4 tsp.	1 pkt.
Apricots	3 lb.	Destone	1 gal.	2 tsp.	2	1 tsp.	2-1/2 lb.	None	1/2 tsp.	1/4 tsp.	1 pkt.
Blackberries	4 lb.	Crush	1 gal.	1 tsp.	2	1 tsp.	2-1/2 lb.	None	1/2 tsp.	None	1 pkt.
Blueberries	2 lb.	Crush	1 gal.	3 tsp.	2	1 tsp. energizer	2-1/2 lb.	1 lb.	1/2 tsp.	None	1 pkt.
Sweet cherries	4 lb.	Crush	1 gal.	3 tsp.	2	1 tsp.	2-1/2 lb.	None	1/2 tsp.	1/4 tsp.	1 pkt.
Sour cherries	3 lb.	Crush	1 gal.	2 tsp.	2	1 tsp.	2-1/2 lb.	None	1/2 tsp.	1/4 tsp.	1 pkt.
Cranberries	4 lb.	Crush	1 gal.	None	2	1 tsp.	3 lb.	1-1/2 lb.	1/2 tsp.	None	1 pkt.
Concord grapes	6 lb.	Crush	1 gal.	None	2	1 tsp.	2-1/2 lb.	None	1/2 tsp.	None	1 pkt.
California grapes	20 lb.	Crush	None	1 tsp.	2	None	None	None	None	None	1 pkt.
Loganberries	2 lb.	Crush	1 gal.	2 tsp.	2	1 tsp.	3 lb.	None	1/2 tsp.	None	1 pkt.
Peaches	3 lb.	Destone	1 gal.	3 tsp.	2	1 tsp.	2-1/2 lb.	None	1/2 tsp.	1/4 tsp.	1 pkt.
Plums	4 lb.	Destone	1 gal.	2 tsp.	2	1 tsp.	2-1/2 lb.	None	1/2 tsp.	1/8 tsp.	1 pkt.
Raspberries	3 lb.	Crush	1 gal.	2 tsp.	2	1 tsp.	2-1/2 lb.	None	1/2 tsp.	1/4 tsp.	1 pkt.
Strawberries	5 lb.	Crush	1 gal.	2 tsp.	2	1 tsp.	2-1/2 lb.	None	1/2 tsp.	1/4 tsp.	1 pkt.

Note: all teaspoon measures in this table are level teaspoons.

Winemaking Suppliers

E. G. Arthurs & Sons, Ltd.
2046 Avenue Road
Toronto, Ontario
Canada M5M 4A6

The Complete Winemaker
1219 Main Street
St. Helena, CA 94574

Danenberger
Food Market
P.O. Box 276P
New Berlin, Il 62670

Great Fermentations
87 Larkspur Street
San Rafael, CA 94901

Oak Barrel Winecraft
1443 Pablo Avenue
Berkley, CA 94702

Semplex of U.S.A.
4159 Thomas Avenue Nort
Minneapolis, MN 55430

Wine-Art of San Diego
460 Fletcher Parkway
El Cajon, CA 92020